Praise for *LIKE SHAKING HANDS WITH GOD*

"A rare thing . . . a book that is more about being than writing."

—*The Hartford Advocate* (CT)

"An enthusiastic conversation about why and how they write. . . . One of those brief dips into the psyche of very good authors that can be so motivating to all of us at various stages of our careers, no matter what we write or aspire to write."

—*American Society of Journalists and Authors Newsletter*

"Here is the transcript of their conversation about where the lives they live meet the art they practice, with candid thoughts on writing, humanity, salvation, art, and the struggle and joy of living."

—*The Writer*

"The authors clearly have a profound respect for each other and for their craft."

—*The Austin Chronicle* (TX)

Like Shaking Hands With God

a conversation about writing

Kurt Vonnegut
&
Lee Stringer

Moderated by Ross Klavan
Foreword by Daniel Simon

Photos by Art Shay

WASHINGTON SQUARE PRESS
PUBLISHED BY POCKET BOOKS
New York London Toronto Sydney Singapore

A Washington Square Press Publication of
POCKET BOOKS, a division of Simon & Schuster, Inc.
1230 Avenue of the Americas, New York, NY 10020

Published by arrangement with Seven Stories Press

For information address Seven Stories Press, 140 Watts Street, New York, NY 10013

ISBN: 0-7434-1058-0

First Washington Square Press trade paperback printing December 2000

10 9 8 7 6 5 4 3 2 1

Cover design by Brigid Pearson
Front cover photos by Art Shay

Printed in the U.S.A.

CONTENTS

"The shoemaker on earth
that had the soul of a poet in him
won't have to make shoes here."

—from *Extract from Captain Stormfield's Visit to Heaven,* by Mark Twain

"Der Wunder hoechstes ist,
Dass uns die wahren, echten Wunder so
Alltaeglich werden koennen, werden sollen."

"The greatest miracle is that true and genuine miracles seem to us banal everyday occurrences."

—from *Nathan Der Weise,* by eighteenth-century poet and critic G. E. Lessing, quoted in *The Writer and Psychoanalysis,* by Edmund Bergler (chapter 3, "Autarchy and Unification," p. 40)

FOREWORD

THE RELATIONSHIP BETWEEN Kurt Vonnegut and Lee Stringer as it has evolved is, I believe, an historic one. Kurt was among the earliest and most loyal of Lee's boosters, comparing him to Jack London and calling his book, *Grand Central Winter*, proof that writers are born, not made. Kurt's enjoyment of Lee's wordplay has been so unbridled that it is as if he were offering his own seat in the Pantheon to this other writer who—sadly for what it says about our country even as it is fortunate for the readers among us—will have to write several other very good books before he is thought of as more than that formerly homeless, formerly crack-addicted guy. The word *former* sticks like glue, and you have to make a million bucks and teach at a university before you really get to start fresh here. Good. We're working on it. And Lee tells me he doesn't think Kurt's writing is too bad either.

The morning after this public conversation, which took place on Thursday, October 1, 1998, at a bookstore on Union Square in Manhattan, Kurt would say it had been a magical evening. And indeed it had, thanks to a wonderful crowd of several hundred bookish, warm-hearted listeners, and these two gracious men.

There is a sentence in a Jewish prayer: A person's thoughts are his or her own, but their expression belongs to God. You feel it in the writings—and the talk—of both these men. As one who believes in the redemptive power of literature, I think Kurt and Lee both write to catch His eye. Neither one of them is taking any chances.

Since its founding, Seven Stories Press has drawn guiding inspiration from two novelists. One, Nelson Algren, believed that literature occurs whenever someone takes up the cause of those whose cases might otherwise be lost, their voices unheard. The other, Kurt Vonnegut, writes that we exist here on Earth to fart around.

I seriously believe them both.

The questions to be asked of Kurt and Lee were prepared beforehand, but were not shared beforehand with either Kurt, Lee, or Ross. Ross was handed two sheets of paper as the public event began, and otherwise supplied his own words as they came to him.

This book came into existence with help from Kurt, Lee, Ross, Paul Abruzzo, Jon Gilbert, Don Farber, Debbie and Dennis of Barnes & Noble, the Café de Paris, Jill Krementz, Art Shay, Agnes Krup for her impromptu assistance with the translation from the German of the G. E. Lessing epigraph, and an audience of truth- and fun-seekers who chose not to stay home on an October evening. Thanks to all.

—Daniel Simon

Brooklyn, May 20, 1999

THE FIRST CONVERSATION

ROSS: Lee and Kurt, why don't you come up so we can grill you. [Kurt Vonnegut and Lee Stringer approach the dais and take their seats.] We'll start with a series of questions and then go into short readings from both books. The first question: You both write about what you know and especially of your personal experiences and adventures. Would you each care to comment on the common ground between you?

KURT: Do you want to do that, Lee?

LEE: I'll defer to you, Kurt.

KURT: The common ground? Well, you have identified it. We have written out of our own lives, and being writers was easier for us because we had something to write about. Thank God I was in Dresden when it was burned down. [Laughter]

Joe Heller said to me one time that if it weren't for World War II he'd be in the dry-cleaning business. I'm not sure what business I would have been in.

LEE: Common ground. That's a tough one. Well, we're both writers. We're both tall.... In reading some of the interviews he has given, one thing he said made me feel we had very much in common. In essence he said that he did his best writing when he really didn't know what he was doing. And I certainly felt like that all during the writing of *Grand Central Winter.*

KURT: When I teach—and I've taught at the Iowa Writers' Workshop for a couple of years, at City College, Harvard—I'm not looking for people who want to be writers. I'm looking for people who are passionate, who care terribly about something. There are people with a hell of a lot on their minds, Lee being a case in point, and if you have a hell of a lot on your mind, the language will arrive, the right words will arrive, the paragraphing will be right. You have the case of Joseph Conrad, for whom English was a third language, and he was passionate in English. The words arrived and formed masterpieces.

ROSS: What are some of the particular challenges that you see facing us today, both literary and human?

KURT: I think nothing has changed. I think the human

situation is like the weather. I look at Yugoslavia, and the world is always going to be that way. You're lucky to be alive, Lee, and I am, too, I think.

LEE: In a way...it's a struggle to be human. I mean, if you really look at it, we wake up every morning to an alien environment. Certainly not the environment man was created in. It's a busy, throbbing, hustling, buzzing, spinning, crazy, alien environment. And the struggle for me, within that, is to try and be human, to try and do human things, to try and remember what we were born with. So to me it is very much a struggle just to be human, not so much a human struggle to do something else, but a struggle just to feel...human.

KURT: And it's important to retreat from the hoopla on television, and what television says matters and what we're all supposed to talk about. And of course literature is the only art that requires our audience to be performers. You have to be able to read and you have to be able to read awfully well. You have to read so well that you get irony! I'll say one thing meaning another, and you'll get it. Expecting a large number of people to be literate is like expecting everybody to play the French horn. It is extremely difficult. And as I've said in this book here [*Timequake*], when we think about what reading is . . . it's impossible. Literature is idiosyncratic arrangements in horizontal lines of only twenty-six phonetic symbols, ten arabic numbers, and about eight punctuation marks. And yet there are people like *you* who can look at a printed page and put on shows in your head—the battle of Waterloo, for God's sake. *The New York Times* says that there are forty million people in the United States who can't read well enough to fill out an application for a driver's license. So our audience cannot be large, because we need a highly skilled audience, unbelievably skilled. . . . Thank you for learning how to do this virtually impossible thing. [Laughter]

LEE: More and more these days I find that people want to boil things down to something simple, something you can grab in a second. I also see that today people are very result-oriented. We don't do anything just because it's the right thing to do, or for the sake of art, or for the sake of anything unless we can prove that down the road x, y, or z is going to happen. I guess in that kind of environment it is difficult for what we call literature to exist because a book is not all that practical a thing in the short term. It's probably infinitely practical in the long term. But you're not going to pick *Timequake* off the shelf and learn how to scramble eggs tomorrow. So, in that context, writing is a struggle to preserve our right to be not so practical....

KURT: When I taught at City College, the students were very upset to find out there was no job at the end of the course.... They couldn't go anyplace and say, well, you know, I studied creative writing at City College and I'd like to write for you....

About "the death of the novel" and so forth: it has never been terribly alive—again, because the audience has to be made up of performers and such an audience is going to be very small.

Bill Styron pointed out one time, in a lecture I was privileged to hear, that the great Russian novels—which were more of an influence on American writers than Hawthorne or Twain or any American writer you'd want to name—were written for very small audiences because the literate population was very small, amid an enormous empire of illiterate people. So Tolstoy, Gogol, and Dostoyevsky were glad to write, even though their audience was small.

ROSS: Given the obstacles, especially the obstacles to reading, is there any reason to be optimistic?

LEE: About?

ROSS: About anything!

KURT: I'm going to die! [Laughter]

LEE: You know, the subject of *Grand Central Winter*, which involves homelessness, has been seen by a lot of people as a tragedy. But usually at the end of a tragedy somebody dies, and being alive right now I can't think of it as a tragedy. What I've taken away is a certain brand of optimism. Even the bad stuff is an opportunity. There are possibilities there. In fact, I see more possibilities in adversity than in, say, lying on satin pillows. So, in that respect, I guess I am an optimist. I think there's reason for optimism—at least for personal optimism. I don't know if the world is going to survive, but I'm going to go as long as my heart beats. [Applause]

KURT: Your book should have political consequences, although you nowhere demand reform. This book should surely be a bestseller in New York City at least, telling us what most of us really had no idea about: what the life of a homeless person is like. Nowhere do you mourn the existence of the homeless. But anybody reading the book is bound to say: My God, something's got to be done about this.

LEE: Um, yeah, well...that's a tough one.

You know, man tries to be a sociologist all the time, but the truth is, you know, if you look around, we really suck at it. So I don't know if there is anything to be done about it [homelessness].

What?

Eliminate it?

Move these people?

Get them out of our faces?

Feed everybody?

I don't know what's to be done about it, except to find what your relationship is to it.

I think that's the only work.

Not to eliminate what offends our sense of what should be, or who we are. Just to find a relationship to it. Just, when you pass somebody on the street: What is your relationship to that person?

I mean, how as human beings do we relate to one another? Anything beyond that is bullshit.

KURT: Lee, you used to sell *Street News*, and you started writing for *Street News*, and then I guess you became probably their top writer. Were you editor-in-chief finally?

LEE: I was editor-in-chief when they decided they couldn't pay any more salaries and everyone else left.

KURT: Yeah, but you got to sleep on the couch in the office!

LEE: Which was a good deal. A great deal.

KURT: I confess I haven't read *Street News* the way I should have. Were there editorials in there about what should be done about the homeless?

LEE: There were some, there were often some. And there was never any accord. It's like trying to push a waterbed flat; you know, you push it here and it pops up over there.

I have a prior history as a subject of applied sociology in being raised black in the sixties. And here it's thirty years later and billions of dollars and lots of speeches and countless laws and all I'm hearing these days is all this has only made things worse so far as black people are concerned. So I really don't have a lot of faith in installing a perfect society or even a pro forma solution to any kind of social problem.

I admit that in those days I wrote a couple of begrudging "I-wish-so-and-so-would-get-off-of-his-this and I-wish-people-would-do-that type of editorials. But, for me, the fun stuff was when I could just riff on my own and just go on about what was inside my head. That was an amazing thing: to be on the streets and not be heard as Joe Homeless but just be able to have a place where I could riff from my own mind. It was a wonderful place to be in the middle of the 1980s. I was rich in that respect. The average person who had a home didn't have that. So it was a remarkable forum for me. Editorials, I always find, are usually about the agenda that gets attached to events, and I got very tired of writing them. I don't suppose I wrote many of them all that well. The stuff I liked was writing about people, places, and things, all that first-person stuff. But I sure loved that couch. [Chuckles from Lee and Kurt]

KURT: Do you run into old friends who are still on the street?

LEE: Yeah, I do.

KURT: And is your impulse to rescue them, or to do something for them?

LEE: Not at all.

KURT: Well, you're not a very nice guy.

LEE: Actually, I'm not very presumptuous either. You know, I barely rescued myself. And one thing I noticed from being on the street is that, looking the other way, all of us are really—everybody in this room—is really just groping their way around in life. We grab on to things that tell us we've got it all figured out, but I bet if I ask for a show of hands of people who have just the littlest bit of doubt that they don't have it all figured out, I bet you everybody would raise their hands. So in that context it would be kind of presumptuous to know you could save the next person—at least for me. This may surprise a lot of people to hear me say it, but it's an honest answer.... Saving myself is going to be a lifetime job, so I don't know if I can really get to the point where I have the time or the wherewithal to save the next guy. I don't know what's right for you. And I wouldn't presume to tell you right now.

KURT: Well, you gave us a wonderful gift in the process of building your soul.

LEE: Thank you.

KURT: I want to say thank you. It's really a swell book. And I compare Lee to Jack London because...Are you going to read the part where Lee realizes he can write?

ROSS: Ahhh...no. That's not part of the plan.

KURT: Well, could you tell the story, Lee? Where were you when you discovered that you really could write?

LEE: Well, I wish I could wiggle out of that one because that's been hammered into the ground. But I was just sitting there with a pencil, I'll say that much. A pencil that I was using as a drug implement, to push the screens in my pipe. And one day I didn't have any drugs and I decided to use it as a pencil. [Laughter] I'm sort of smart that way. Because I was going to use that pencil some way or another, I guess. And I started writing. And the extraordinary thing was that it was five hours later before I stopped. I don't think I had done anything for five hours in a row during that time *except* try to get high or try to outrun the effects of getting high. I don't think there was anything else that

I did with that much concentration. It was a real moment.

KURT: I identifed Lee with Jack London originally because Jack London had the same sort of experience. He had hit bottom and he was working in a steam laundry. And he decided, God, there's [got to be] something better than this. And he started writing. And it turned out he could *really do it*....

Ask us a question. [Laughter]

ROSS: I think this is a good place to read a little bit from each of the books.

The first passage is from *Grand Central Winter.*

[Ross reads aloud:]

Hell's Kitchen, Fall 1994. *It's one of those bright, glorious Indian-summer days, gold dust streaming through the front windows of the* Street News *editorial office, the treetops across Ninth Avenue swaying gently in the breeze. I'm standing hunched over my desk, teeth clenched, cursing and muttering at the printer—one of those worthless,* *low-end Panasonic dot-matrix jobs with a temperament all its own—sitting in frozen silence, red "error" light blinking dumbly back at me, refusing to print so much as a digit. And what keeps running through my mind is, Why am I doing this?*

But I know why.

I did it to myself.

I went and got myself an honest job.

Not that I was looking. I had an income. I sold papers. As many and for as long as my needs required. I didn't really feel I was missing anything out of life by being on the street either—at least not anything that could be had by a paycheck. And I wasn't really interested in being employed simply for the sake of it. What I wanted was to do something worth a bit of satisfaction as well as a buck. Something that might make a difference.

...

I imagined that as a writer I might help light up Street News*'s pages and that this might help it emerge from its doldrums.*

I was wrong of course.

Not that I'm complaining exactly. I enjoy work-

ing with words. That part of the job delivers a certain satisfaction. But as for any of my work making a real difference in the larger scheme of things, as for it having any impact on the growing public resentment toward homeless people, for example, I have had to climb down from that high horse.

From *Timequake*:
[Ross reads aloud:]

I have taught creative writing during my seventy-three years on automatic pilot, rerun or not. I did it first at the University of Iowa in 1965. After that came Harvard, and then the City College of New York. I don't do it anymore.

I taught how to be sociable with ink on paper. I told my students that when they were writing they should be good dates on blind dates, should show strangers good times. Alternatively, they should run really nice whorehouses, come one, come all, although they were in fact working in perfect solitude. I said I expected them to do this with nothing but idosyncratic arrangements in horizontal lines of twenty-

six phonetic symbols, ten numbers, and maybe eight punctuation marks, because it wasn't anything that hadn't been done before.

In 1996, with movies and TV doing such good jobs of holding the attention of literates and illiterates alike, I have to question the value of my very strange, when you think about it, charm school. There is *this: Attempted seductions with nothing but words on paper are so* cheap *for would-be-ink-stained Don Juans or Cleopatras! They don't have to get a bankable actor or actress to commit to the project, and then a bankable director, and so on, and then raise millions and millions of buckareenies from manic-depressive experts on what most people want.*

Still and all, why bother? Here's my *answer: Many people need desperately to receive this message: "I feel and think much as you do, care about many of the things you care about, although most people don't care about them. You are not alone."*

[Applause]

ROSS: So that leads to the question: Why do we do what we do, either writing or anything else?

LEE: Well, since you've billed me as the new Jack London, I'll have to say it beats working in a laundry. [Laughter]

For me, the reason I do it is it's the first thing I completely chose to do on my own: tried on my own, made up myself, and kind of found that I could do all right at it. That's almost ninety percent of it. I guess there's ten percent in the fact that I find that it's very good for me. So that leaves maybe half a percent where I hope it'll be good for you guys. I don't mean to be stingy, but I found that when I try to do it the other way, I overdo it, and then it's good for no one.

KURT: There's a swell book that's out of print now. Maybe Seven Stories will bring it out again. It's called *The Writer and Psychoanalysis* by a man who's now dead named Edmund Bergler. He claimed he had treated more writers than anyone else in his field, and being that he practiced in New York, he probably did. Bergler said that writers were fortunate in that they were able to treat their neuroses every day by writing. He also said that as soon as a writer was blocked, this was catastrophic because the writer would start to go to pieces. And so I said in a piece in *Harper's*, or a letter I wrote to *Harper's*, about "the death of the novel": *People will continue to write novels, or maybe short stories, because they discover that they are treating their own neuroses.* And I have said about the practice of the arts that practicing any art—be it painting, music, dance, literature, or whatever—is not a way to make money or become famous. *It's a way to make your soul grow.* So you should do it *anyway*. [Applause] And what Bill Gates is saying now.... How much were they offering to kill Salman Rushdie?

SOMEONE FROM THE AUDIENCE: A million dollars.

KURT: I'll pay anybody here a million dollars who'll kill Bill Gates. [Laughter]

LEE: Let's see the money.

KURT: Gates is saying, "Hey, don't worry about making your soul grow. I'll sell you a new program and, instead, let your computer grow year after year after year..."—cheating people out of the experience of becoming.

LEE: You know, I saw a book review in one of the papers today and the book was about how to hold on to power, how to be powerful. On the face of it it seems like a go-go nineties book, but when you think about it, some of the advice he was giving people in the book was totally antihuman: Make people depend on you. [Laughter] People run out to buy books to learn how to do this. One of his points was, "Don't say much. People will think you're smart."

I wondered why he wrote the book. [Laughter]

So when you're shooting Bill Gates, if your bullet misses, I hope it hits this guy. [Laughter]

ROSS: We have another passage, this one from *Grand Central Winter*. Afterward, we'll ask more questions. This describes an encounter in a Central Booking holding cell.

[Ross reads aloud:]

Early that evening the cell gates clanged open and the CO ushered in a thin, bare-chested Spanish kid wearing hospital-green pajama bottoms splattered with crimson. His arms were swathed, wrist to elbow, in bandages and he was grinning ear to ear.

"They had to keep my shirt for evidence," he announced to no one in particular, holding his damaged arms aloft like trophies. Then, without prompting, he launched, with relish, into his war story. He and his crew were doing a burglary... the cops had surprised them in the middle of it... he "took a bullet" in one arm trying to escape (a matter of particular pride) and had done-in the other arm scrambling over razor wire. They had to patch him up at Bellevue before they could book him. All in all, a Hollywood-worthy night out for a restless teen.

"They tell me I'm a career criminal," he gushed, "in-curr-ridge-i-ble."

Everyone was duly impressed. I was both captivated and unsettled by his moxy, though I never let on....

I was puffing on a cigarette, contemplating how much of it to leave for the guy who had begged the "short" from me, when I saw The Kid move for the Jersey boy.

"I like that rope, homeboy," he said, leaning his face into Jersey's. "Let me get that chain!" Something in his hand was pressing against Jersey's jugular.

Incorrigible.

This was just the thing to break the monotony of sitting on your butt awaiting the pleasure of the court. The holding cell sprang to life. A circle of inmates formed two-deep around Jersey and The Kid. If we were going to be treated to a throw-down, they were determined to keep the COs at bay for as long as possible.

But Jersey had had enough fisticuffs for one night, apparently. He didn't give up the chain. But he did yell for help. I heard keys rattle in the gate. A second later, correction officers were elbowing their way through the human blockade. But The Kid, who could have easily ditched the shiv, remained oblivious to them. He just stood there menacing Jersey while the guards broke through and grabbed him.... And as they hauled him off to book him on an additional charge, I caught a glimpse of his face.

His smirk was wider than ever.

Most of us in the cell could expect to walk. We knew if we just bided our time and let the criminal justice grind take its course, we could get back to whatever it was we were doing with a minimum of hassle. The Kid, though, knew he wasn't going anywhere. He was a "career criminal." He also knew that with his good looks, youth, and diminutive size, it was better to go inside with a "don't-give-a-fuck" badass rep preceding him. In that respect he was, for all his bravado, only being practical, and buying in on the cheap for all that.

...

When it comes to justice, the kind that gets you locked up is different from the kind you find inside. Personally I would like to see all judges and district attorneys made to do time. Not for the crimes they commit from the bench. For they commit those out of ignorance. Which is precisely why time in prison should be part of their qualifications. So that they might come to know what they don't know they don't know.

Let them sit faceless and despised in the holding cells, let them be run through the wringer of their process until the wind has been wrung out of their self-righteousness. And let them stumble on the wisdom every two-bit con knows instinctively, that real justice is always poetic.

[Applause]

ROSS: The question is: There is *the adventure* of life and there is *our need to understand* the adventure of life. What might be the relationship between those two events for each of you?

LEE: Wow.

KURT: I'm still kind of flummoxed here because Lee writes better than I do. [Laughter]

LEE: Well, I'll take a shot at that.... The big questions like that make me nervous because it took quite a while to write this book and now it's all packaged and it's out there...so I don't want to say anything that's going to fuck it up. [Laughter]

Right now I've got everybody's confidence because of the book.... For me, to answer your question, there is a very, very, very big relationship. What did you call it? The adventure? I did look at my time on the street as an adventure. I looked at it that way from the very first day. I said, "Well, let's see what happens next." When I finally came up for air...Actually I made a big mistake. I don't think the mistake was the streets. I think it was getting myself trapped all over again. It wasn't any particular thing, but at the time I got myself trapped, I was trapped in a certain cycle. And once I got off the streets, I didn't know what else to do with myself. I certainly didn't want to be back in this nonexistent thing called the mainstream!

And it was only the book.... I sat there for about a year and a half hoping to finish it. And the relationship was that I couldn't finish it until I resolved a few things. I mean I despise pure exposition, just putting down the details—"On October fourth I did this, then that happened"—I can't stand doing that. I can't sit down and do that. There are writers who can do that, reporters who can do that very well. I'd rather have my teeth drilled.

So I had to find a way to write it and reasons to write it that were interesting to me and, hopefully, worth your time.

It never occurred to me that anybody walking past a bookstore would be particularly interested in what this unknown person named Lee Stringer had to say. But if I was lucky enough for somebody to happen to pick up a book I'd written and browse through it, I wanted to make sure that they felt they'd got a good thing and might even want to continue reading it.

So out of that process I found that I couldn't find a way into any of the episodes in the book until I understood what each one meant to me. Not only what the people around me were doing but why. So by the end of the writing of this book I had answered a whole bunch of questions. And I thought that was a very wonderful thing.

Having it published is almost an afterthought in that respect. For me, the top of the mountain was answering those questions for myself.

ROSS: All right, well let's cause some more trouble with the final selection. This is from *Timequake*:

[Ross reads aloud:]

A Luddite to the end, as was Kilgore Trout, as was Ned Ludd, the possibly but not certainly fictitious workman who smashed up machinery, supposedly, in Leicestershire, England, at the beginning of the nineteenth century, I persist in pecking away at a manual typewriter. That still leaves me technologically several generations ahead of William Styron and Stephen King, who, like Trout, write with pens on yellow legal pads.

I correct my pages with pen or pencil. I have come into Manhattan on business. I telephone a woman who has been doing my retyping for years and years now. She doesn't have a computer, either. Maybe I should can her. She has moved from the city to a country town. I ask her what the weather is like out that way. I ask if there have been any unusual birds at her bird feeder. I ask if squirrels have found a way to get at it, and so on.

Yes, the squirrels have found a new way to get at

the feeder. They can become trapeze artists, if they have to.

She has had back trouble in the past. I ask her how her back is. She says her back is OK. She asks how my daughter Lily is. I say Lily is OK. She asks how old Lily is now, and I say she'll be fourteen in December.

She says, "Fourteen! My gosh, my gosh. It seems like only yesterday she was just a little baby."

I say I have a few more pages for her to type. She says, "Good." I will have to mail them to her, since she doesn't have a fax. Again: Maybe I should can her.

I am still on the third floor of our brownstone in the city, and we don't have an elevator. So down the stairs I go with my pages, clumpity, clumpity, clumpity. *I get down to the first floor, where my wife has her office. Her favorite reading when she was Lily's age was stories about Nancy Drew, the girl detective.*

Nancy Drew is to Jill what Kilgore Trout is to me, so Jill says, "Where are you going?"

I say, "I am going to buy an envelope."

She says, "You are not a poor man. Why don't you buy a thousand envelopes and put them in a closet?" She thinks she is being logical. She has a computer. She has a fax. She has an answering machine on her telephone, so she doesn't miss any important messages. She has a Xerox. She has all that garbage.

I say, "I'll be back real soon."

. . .

Out into the world I go! Muggers! Autograph hounds! Junkies! People with real jobs! Maybe an easy lay! United Nations functionaries and diplomats!

. . .

Into the news store I go. Relatively poor people, with lives not strikingly worth living, are lined up to buy lottery tickets or other crap. [Laughter] *All keep their cool. They pretend they don't know I'm a celebrity.* [Laughter]

The store is a Ma-and-Pa joint owned by Hindus, *honest-to-God* Hindus! *The woman has a teeny-weeny ruby between her eyes. That's worth a trip. Who needs an envelope?*

You must remember this, a kiss is still a kiss, a sigh is still a sigh.

I know the Hindus' stock of stationery as well as they do. I didn't study anthropology for nothing. I find one nine-by-twelve manila envelope without assistance, remembering simultaneously a joke about the Chicago Cubs baseball team. The Cubs were supposedly moving to the Philippine Islands, where they would be renamed the Manila Folders. That would have been a good joke about the Boston Red Sox, too.

I take my place at the end of the line, chatting with fellow customers who are buying something other than lottery tickets. The lottery-ticket suckers, decorticated by hope and numerology, may as well be victims of Post-Timequake Apathy. You could run them over with an eighteen-wheeler. They wouldn't care.

...

From the news store I go one block south to the Postal Convenience Station, where I am secretly in love with a woman behind the counter. I have already put my pages in the manila envelope. I address it, and then I take my place at the end of another long line. What I need now is postage! Yum, yum, yum!

The woman I love there does not know I love her. You want to talk about poker faces? When her eyes meet mine, she might as well be looking at a cantaloupe!

. . .

I put the waiting time to good use. I learn about stupid bosses and jobs I will never have, and about parts of the world I will never see, and about diseases I hope I will never have, and about different kinds of dogs people have owned, and so on. By means of a computer? No. I do it by means of the lost art of conversation.

I at last have my envelope weighed and stamped by the only woman in the whole wide world who could make me sincerely happy. . . .

I go home. I have had one heck of a good time. Listen: We are here on Earth to fart around. [Laughter] *Don't let anybody tell you any different!*

[Laughter and prolonged applause]

ROSS: Which leads to the next question, which is: Do you think there's a place beyond the text that readers experience when they read you, and if so what is that place beyond the words you write?

KURT: Well, as I've said, our readers have to be performers, so they themselves have done work in order to decode these messages on the page. Because they are involved, they become our partners. They've brought themselves to it. That's the extra dimension about which we know nothing. But it's delightful to know that they can bring themselves to it. They have to, or they can't read.

LEE: I don't know quite how to say it.... Maybe I can tell it in a story. I sense there's another dimension, but I can't quite nail it down. But I can tell this story, which may get us near there: One day while I was on the street, I was walking down Forty-second Street between Eighth and Ninth Avenues. It was the middle of the afternoon. It was kind of a gray day. And what I had coming toward me was a marching army, people just slogging along in the middle of the day. Nobody was smiling. Everybody was walking, eyes straight ahead, going to wherever they were going or coming from wherever they'd been. And if you really looked at it, they were all suffering. It was a burden just to go through what was their day.

As I got near the end of the block, I heard the tinkle of a piano and I saw above all these gray heads this one pink sort of melon-shaped thing going like this [gestures in a bouncing, swaying motion], and as I got nearer the corner I found it was a preacher from Jersey who had set up these huge speakers on the end of Forty-second Street, which I call God's Corner, and he was playing this very bright, very modern gospel music in the middle of this very gray, very sad kind of day. And he was just leaping up and down with joy and—no reason for it—he had just set up these speakers and was leaping about, shimmering with pink-faced iridescence. And I said to myself, God, now *that's* where I want to be, where this guy is.

And you know, in a less direct way I'd like people to just sort of read and say, "Well, you know, *that's* where I'd like to be." As simple as that. [Prolonged applause]

KURT: I just want to add that virtually every writer I know would rather be a musician. [Laughter]

ROSS: Why?

KURT: Because music gives pleasure as we never can. Music is the most pleasurable and magical thing we can experience. [Applause]

I'm Honorary President of the American Humanist Association, but I simultaneously say that music is the proof of the existence of God. [Prolonged applause]

ROSS: Do you play an instrument, by the way?

KURT: I play the clarinet badly. I really have no gift for it whatsoever. And I'll tell you, our president is no bad reed man. He's not bad. I've heard him play. Yet nobody has brought that up in his defense. [Laughter]

LEE: That man can really blow, so to speak. [Laughter] Sorry. [Applause]

ROSS: What do you think is the relationship, say, between Kurt Vonnegut and Lee Stringer sitting here and the writers that the reader encounters in your books?

LEE: Wow, that's a tough question. I don't know.... You go first.

KURT: Well, one nice thing about our trade, as compared with poetry or with painting, possibly with music, is we don't envy each other. James McNeil Whistler, a painter, said, "If you wish to see envy, go among the painters." Novelists do not envy each other, and if a writer succeeds, makes a lot of money, say, that makes all other writers happy.

So it's a most agreeable field we're in and I think, in a sense, we are veterans of the same battle and we know what the hell it was like. We're not like Duke Wayne, who was never in a battle. We know what that fight was like and we respect each other for making it.

And anyone who has finished a book, whether the thing has been published or not, whether the thing is any good or not, is a colleague of ours.

LEE: I read Kurt's books years ago. I never wanted to be trendy, so I read them just after everybody else read them. Then I was sorry I'd waited so long. [Laughter]

When I heard that Kurt liked my book, it was like meeting a comrade. To have another writer speak favorably about your work is just a great feeling.

This is not a science. We're not making porcelain. We're not cutting out two-by-fours. It's kind of crazy stuff to just sit in a room and click away at a—in my case, if you'll forgive me, a Mac—for eight or nine hours. It is a very unnatural thing to do. And there's no one there to tell you whether what you're doing is right or wrong. It's a very scary thing, to spend a year or so doing that. And the real fear is that you'll look back and say, "Gee I've wasted a year doing nothing." So in the midst of that loneliness to have another writer say, "You know, you did all right," is a great thing. In that respect I feel like Kurt is a comrade for life. And then, rereading some of his stuff, reading some of his interviews, hearing his comments, I thought we were real comrades.

There is something that a lot of writers, including Kurt, James Baldwin, Ralph Ellison, and Nelson

Algren, do.... There is something we all do that's similar. We sort of futz about in saying what that is, yet I can hear it resonating in the work of all these people. So I overworked that little thought. But thank you for listening. [Applause]

KURT: I always liked Jacqueline Susann, whom I considered a colleague. She wrote with utter sincerity, or people would not have bought her books.

You cannot fool a reading audience!

She was sincere about storytelling and a very nice thing happened between Jacqueline Susann and myself before we met. *Valley of the Dolls* was number one on the bestseller list for, I don't know, two years, something like that. Entertained a lot of people. And I finally knocked her off with *Breakfast of Champions*, which was very briefly number one on the bestseller list. [Applause] And I got a note from this woman, who was a stranger at that time. She said, "As long as it had to be someone, I'm glad it was you." Isn't that graceful? [Applause]

ROSS: You spoke of Lee before as a born writer. Do you feel that you were a born writer as well?

KURT: I don't know. Yes, I think so. Because some people are born musicians, some people are born chess players, or whatever. In school some people could run a lot faster than I could. I could write better than most people could. So, yes, I'm lucky.

Joe Heller and I recently confessed something which is shameful for writers to confess. We'd both had relatively happy childhoods [Laughter], which is no way for a writer to begin. [Prolonged laughter]

What about yours, Lee? It's none of my business....

LEE: Um, you know, it was happy to me. It was happy to me. I was angry. But I was happy at the same time.

KURT: I understand that.

LEE: I wasn't satisfied. Maybe that played a part.

But you know I tried to write a few times when I was younger, but it was never about anything. I mean I liked to play with words, I certainly liked to read a lot. But it was never about anything that I knew anything about. It was always about, you know, spies, and trips to outer space, and things I didn't know anything about, and it had nothing to do with any characters, so I'd get a great first paragraph.... I have a trunkful of first paragraphs somewhere that might become a book one day if I get lucky.

KURT: You want some tips on writing? [Laughter]

LEE: Sure.

Well, you know, I had a lot of fun bumping into... It's a joy of discovery for me. I kind of would not like to know what I'm doing.

I had a lot of fun trying to figure out how I was going to fill up these pages, and then, convinced that I'm not going to figure it out, bingo! something happens. It's like shaking hands with God. It's really a great payoff for the hours you sit around wondering if you can do what you're trying to do.

KURT: Once again, a proof of God, I think. Sculptors, of course, feel that somebody else is using their hands, that they couldn't possibly be doing this. Anyway, the arts are so good to those who practice them.

LEE: I wanted to ask you, now that I have you here. I wanted to talk to you in private, but I haven't had the chance. So there's this one question I wanted to ask you. [Laughter] Do you find when you're writing, you get to a point where it's almost like taking dictation?

KURT: Ah, well I have to think about that. Ah, yeah in a way. I'd never thought about that image before. Yes, I guess so. I feel I'm lucky as hell. Here it is again. I can't really do this. Somebody else must be doing this, like taking dictation. But again, I've written a hell of a lot of crap. I'm glad I didn't publish most of it. But there it was. I'd write for three or four hours, or all day, and: "This is lousy." Have you ever done that?

LEE: Absolutely. [Laughter] There are two other *Grand Central Winter*s in the drawer.

ROSS: So this may be a good place to end. Kurt Vonnegut, Lee Stringer, thank you very much for coming. The books are *Grand Central Winter* and *Timequake.*

[Very long applause]

VOICES IN THE CROWD: Thank you.... Yeah.... Huh? Did you? Hi. One more?... You were great!... Yeah! Ah, yes. Did you get my book?... I am. My son was. Yes. Huh?

KURT: Yeah, we both are.

LEE: What does that tell us? Oh...Scorpio run amok!

KURT: Also, they're full of secrets, aren't they?

VOICES: Totally. Yeah. Here, here you go. Enjoy your life.

LEE: I once heard someone say, speaking of secrets, you're only as sick as your secrets. Absolutely true. Absolutely! True.

VOICE IN THE CROWD: Mr. Vonnegut, are you going to write another book?

KURT: Look, I'm...He's...How old are you, Lee? Are you forty-two?

LEE: Forty-seven.

KURT: Forty-seven? I'm twice as old as he is. Why should I write another thing?

VOICE IN THE CROWD: I just wondered, because I know you said *Timequake* was your last—

KURT: No, they're bringing out a collection of short stories that were never collected. And that will be the end. All I'll write is a new preface....

THE SECOND CONVERSATION

(In early January 1999, Kurt, Lee, Ross, and Dan met for lunch at the Café de Paris, a neighborhood restaurant in New York City, where they were able to smoke and pick up some of the threads of their earlier conversation in a more private setting. The conversation took a darker, more serious turn, and more hopeful, too, in the sense that any attempts to talk about unweildy matters are essentially optimistic endeavors.—ed.)

ROSS: Reading both you guys—and it is also true talking to you—I feel smarter, as opposed, say, to reading the newspaper, which can make any of us feel stupid and helpless. I wondered if that was something you could comment on?

KURT: Well, you know, both of us were born to write what we wrote—and God help us economically. There wasn't much we could do to fine-tune ourselves. There are some people who can, I guess; Clancy, and others. But we were doomed to write what we wrote and, ah, we lucked out with a public.

LEE: You know, after [*Grand Central Winter*] was published, I had a hard time writing anything that made any sense. And I realized this was because at all the readings people asked a lot of questions. And after all those questions you begin to form answers, to draw conclusions. I discovered that, in my case anyway, the writing comes out of, you know, the questions...trying to find an answer. The process of writing helps me do that in a way that readers can follow along. And that may be why they might feel smarter: It's not something I already know and am feeding down to them. I'm making the trip with them.

KURT: Yeah, but you lucked out in terms of who you are.

LEE: Right?

KURT: You don't put the reader on a guilt trip.

LEE: Right. Absolutely.

KURT: Because this person doesn't have to read the goddamn book, you know. You don't say, Look you dumb motherfuckers, this is what it was like for us to be out on the street! And what are you gonna do about it? And all that.

LEE: Uh-huh.

KURT: And you might have done that, but you didn't. Because of who you are.

LEE: Well, you know, I spent a lot of time on the subways selling *Street News.* Every three minutes there's somebody coming through telling people how victimized they are....

ROSS: Kurt, now that Lee is facing the prospect of writing his second and third books, do you have advice or counsel or—?

KURT: [Turning to Lee] You don't have to write it.

LEE: Oh.... [Laughing]

KURT: No, really.

LEE: [Still laughing] I don't have to write it.

KURT: Yeah. No, but I mean it.

LEE: Uh-huh.

KURT: That could be your release. And so, you write it because you want to—if you want to. You don't want to write a second book? You don't know if you can.

LEE: That's a very interesting thought....

ROSS: I like that. It reminds me of NBA coach Phil Jackson. When it looked like upstart Indiana might win the playoffs last year, Phil Jackson said to his team, "We might lose." That was very important to say.

LEE: You know what I think my problem is? I know things I shouldn't know now. I know the afterward stuff. What Barnes and Noble is doing, how Oprah might respond, what stores put up front and what they don't put up front. Even with the first book it was more a process of clearing things out of the way, so I hate to sit down and think of Oprah and marketability. None of those things should be on your mind.

KURT: I hope they're not.

LEE: Well, they... they crawl in there. Now, part of the job for me is to get that cleared away.

KURT: Well, how much... You're gonna sell your body now? It's easier to turn to prostitution.

LEE: Well, maybe at a younger age... maybe with a better body! [Laughter] You know, it's not that conscious, but... somebody said to me once, "Fuck the audience! Write what you want to write." But to me it's a conversation: You have to be talking to somebody.

KURT: Look, you've already found out you were born knowing how to talk to the audience. So you don't need to learn that. If you write an insincere book, the reader will see right through you. And you take a schlock writer like Jacqueline Susann, who wrote *Valley of the Dolls*, she was a colleague of ours and her books have sold because the reader can see she meant it—

LEE: —Uh-huh.

KURT: There was no way [for her] to write an insincere, calculated book. All a writer has to do is write one book, and you did that. Look, how old are you now?

LEE: Ah . . . forty-eight.

KURT: In the Middle Ages you'd be dead!

LEE: Yeah, that's right. I would, wouldn't I.

KURT: And François Villon's reputation survives to the present day on the basis of a thousand lines of poetry—

LEE: —Uh-huh.

KURT: That's it.

LEE: So, "Quit while you're ahead."

KURT: No, not "quit while you're ahead." You've paid your dues, for Christ's sake.

LEE: Uhm.

KURT: I'm just telling you, you've done enough—

LEE: I don't owe anybody anything—

KURT: —You've done enough, yeah.

LEE: That's good. I...see.... I'm gonna use that line....

ROSS: Of course, when this gets transcribed, it's gonna be: "Keep on writing, Lee! Don't give up!" [Laughter]

KURT: The space between my first and second book was ten years.

LEE: Ah!

KURT: Then I went to a cocktail party here in New York. I talked to an editor there and he asked me what I was doing. I told him. It just came pouring out: *The Sirens of Titan*. That was my second book. Just came. *Brrrrr*. Just like a doorbell. *BRRRRR-ah*.

LEE: It just occurred to you at that time, or the title just—

KURT: It had been cooking up here the whole time [Taps his temple].

LEE: Exactly! Now, I know that feeling. In fact I think the last thing you do is sit down at the keyboard.... That's the last act. A whole bunch of other stuff has to happen first.

ROSS: What are some truths that you think a writer should not reveal?

KURT: Well, again, it's about being a good blind

date.... And what are you gonna tell your blind date? "Actually, I'm very insecure.... I'm uneasy tonight...and I hope we get along good?" Not likely.

ROSS: Is writing a form of public speaking?

KURT: Partly it's about how you hold an audience. Because they can leave.

LEE: Well, that's a tough question for me. I don't know yet. I suppose it'll be a while before I—

KURT: —Nobody gives a fuck about you. They care about the book.

LEE: But in terms of the question he asked...about what should or should not be revealed....

KURT: Now we're talking politics.... There was a time, if you were gay, you would cut out anything in the book that would give that away. Because gays were hated. And you don't want the reader, no matter what a prick he or she may be, to hate you.

LEE: Huh. That's true.

KURT: But that's no longer a consideration.

LEE: Well, I guess it would depend on what the book was. You can reveal some things in some books that you wouldn't reveal—for the sake of your voice—in another book. Wouldn't that be true?

KURT: Are we talking about fiction or journalism?

LEE: Well, the question didn't specify.

KURT: Well, in one you reveal everything—

ROSS: Which one is that?

KURT: In journalism.

In fiction, it's like being a magician. And saying it's not fair to the audience because I didn't really levitate this woman. [Laughter]

In Roth's novel *The Ghostwriter*, Anne Frank should have stayed alive. Because it's the nature of an experiment. You run it out to the end. He double-crossed the reader, spoiled the story.

When I was writing short stories for slick magazines—it was true of my novels too—I never knew how to end them. And my agent said, "It's perfectly simple, my boy: The hero gets on his horse and rides into the sunset."

That's what Anne Frank should have done. I think it would have been beautiful. We'd still be talking about that book if he had had her stay among us.

One time I was talking to a guy about a book I was working on, it was about Alger Hiss, and Hiss was sitting there [He points]. I didn't realize it. And just the other night I was with Martin Garbus, the lawyer, and we started talking about Hiss, and we both agreed about something which neither of us had ever admitted to anybody before: Yes, he did give small bits of information to the Soviet Union, but it was part of the romance of the times. But you hate to do that....

I have trouble with evolution, but I'm not gonna tell anybody [Laughs].

LEE: One of those things that you don't reveal, I guess....

KURT: Well, that's politics.

ROSS: Is there a right relationship for a writer to have with social issues and as a person of conscience?

KURT: I was always interested in good citizenship. It was just what I learned in junior civics class in school in Indianapolis, how important it is to be a good citizen. Part of that would be, with me, that I would go to war, right or wrong. I would have gone to Vietnam, knowing how wrong it was.

LEE: You know, when I first met Greg [Greg Ruggiero, an activist and publisher], he asked me, "Are you an activist?" And I kind of hemmed and hawed on it. And he walked away disappointed. But it occurred to me afterward that before you had the guys marching, you had the people who reported on the poverty and the war.... Before the action there has to be the question. I just have more fun playing around with the questions.

ROSS: Do you think that if we lived in a better world, or if the world rehabilitated itself a little bit, would that be an inspiration to writers?

KURT: I think it would be fun because we would be like the founding fathers on the edge of a virgin continent. And out of this came the Bill of Rights, by the way.

LEE: The whole concept of the world rehabilitating itself escapes me, but the question is: Can you write anything on Park Avenue, really? And I'm living in the middle of a suburb right now and I certainly hope you're able to. I'm finding it easier to write the personal stuff now. But the condition of the world, as far as I'm concerned, is always about the personal stuff. We put it up on a big scale, but it's *really* about the personal stuff.

ROSS: What would be a good subject for a novel today or tomorrow?

KURT: Partly because I'm an anthropologist, I would write about pulling the wall down in Germany, the mingling of these two cultures. They closed the factories in East Germany because they were inefficient, producing forty percent unemployment. They're all boarded up now because they have new owners in West Germany, and the United States, too, I imagine. For Christ's sake, this is like taking away the Indians' teepees.

Anthropologists should have been in there first. I'd ask, "Are these factories inefficient?" The cheapest thing the West Germans can do now is help keep them running. Instead of social services coming in to house these people, instead of skinheads, hell, it'd just be the factory where they'd been working anyway.

ROSS: Lee?

LEE: I don't have any plot lines or scenarios, really, but there are two themes that keep popping up, two things I heard that I can't let go of. One is, "You're only as sick as your secrets." I like that. And the other is, "The door to hell is locked from the inside." They're not my concepts, but they just resounded when I heard them. I'm not sure how to put them into a novel yet, or what the faces will look like.... I mean, most of us don't so much want to go to heaven as not go to hell. So, I think, from that point of view—

KURT: Have you read *Captain Stormfield's Visit to Heaven*?

ROSS: What's that?

KURT: One of the last books Twain wrote. This Mississippi River pilot finally dies and, ah, he goes to heaven. He's given a harp and—

LEE: —Oh, I remember this one.

KURT: He sits on a cloud. And he says, "Well, what's goin' on?" Well, there's going to be a parade. Okay, he'll go watch the parade. And so here the parade comes and these people are marching in order of rank. And there's Abraham and there's Jesus and there's Muhammad, leading. Behind them it's Shakespeare, and the great writers of all time. Then there's a little guy marching all by himself. Stormfield was able to identify the others, but he's got to ask who the little guy is. And it turns out this guy is the greatest writer who ever lived. He's a tailor, a Jewish tailor from Tennessee. And he wrote, and threw everything he wrote in a trunk. And one night a bunch of ruffians decided to have fun with this guy. And they tarred and feathered him, rode him out of town on a rail, just for fun, threw him in a ditch, and he died of pneumonia. And his wife hated him, was ashamed of him, and burned the trunk.

* * *

LEE: The picture we paint of heaven is of something always beyond ourselves, filled with things that are nice, but which we're not interested in...and that's how we can keep ourselves locked into this concept of hell. I think that's the whole point. Drawing that line.

KURT: Okay, Lee, you've died.

LEE: Yeah.

KURT: And you are given this option: Do you want to sleep for eternity, or do you want to go back to Earth?

LEE: Uh-huh.

KURT: So what're you gonna do?

LEE: Well, I can answer the question, but I don't see that as being a—

KURT: —Well, [Laughing] fuck you!

LEE: —heaven-and-hell thing.

DAN: That's like Hamlet.

LEE: Hell is eternal. You carry it with you.

DAN: Do I get to dream? If I get to dream, I'll sleep. If not, of course I'll go back to Earth.

KURT: All right, that's nice. Never thought to ask that. Good answer.

LEE: If you can presume that heaven is sleep, which nobody's proven to me yet, uhm, then I might want to come back to Earth. But that's just it. Assuming that heaven's just this blank, eternal sleep, you know, is one way of keeping yourself in hell.

KURT: It would be absolutely okay with me.

LEE: Eternal sleep?

KURT: Yes.

LEE: All right.

KURT: I really like sleep. [Laughter]

LEE: Oh! I like sleep. I like sleep when I'm waking up.

KURT: No, but he came up with the right answer. I really was counting on dreaming. And that—

LEE: —Then you have to choose your dreams.

KURT: No, I'll take 'em as they come. I haven't really had any really bad ones. Have you?

LEE: Oh, I've had bad dreams. Not many lately.... I used to have a recurring dream of being in an airplane that's about to crash—right in the cockpit—about to crash. And you know it's about to crash and it keeps wavering....

* * *

KURT: Lee, I never asked you, but what kind of education did you have?

LEE: Just high school, but it was a good one.

KURT: That's the story of my life too. I went to a good high school, and everything was noise after that.

* * *

That tailor Billings, from Tennessee, wrote poetry that Homer and Shakespeare couldn't begin to come up to; but nobody would print it, nobody read it but his neighbors, an ignorant lot, and they laughed at it. Whenever the village had a drunken frolic and a dance, they would drag him in and crown him with cabbage leaves, and pretend to bow down to him; and one night when he was sick and nearly starved to death, they had him out and crowned him, and then they rode him on a rail about the village, and everybody followed along, beating tin pans and yelling. Well, he died before morning. He wasn't ever expecting to go to heaven, much less that there was going to be any fuss made over him.... Well, anyway, Billings had the grandest reception that has been seen in thousands of centuries.... Why, look here—Shakespeare walked backwards before that tailor from Tennessee, and scattered flowers for him to walk on, and Homer stood behind his chair and waited on him at the banquet.... I wish there was something in *that miserable spiritualism, so we could send them word. That Tennessee village would set up a monument to Billings, then, and his autograph would outsell Satan's.*

—from Mark Twain's *Extract from Captain Stormfield's Visit to Heaven,* pp. 87–96

BIBLIOGRAPHY

Stringer, Lee. *Grand Central Winter: Stories from the Street.* New York: Seven Stories Press, 1998.

Vonnegut, Kurt. *Timequake.* New York: G. P. Putnam's Sons, 1997.

BOOKS MENTIONED IN THE CONVERSATIONS:

Bergler, M.D., Edmund. *The Writer and Psychoanalysis*, 2d ed. Madison, Conn.: International Universities Press, 1992, p. 40.

Roth, Philip. *The Ghost Writer.* New York: Vintage, 1995.

Susann, Jacqueline. *Valley of the Dolls.* Reprint, New York: Grove Atlantic, 1997. (For a biography of Jacqueline Susann, we recommend *Lovely Me: The Life of Jacqueline Susann* by Barbara Seaman. Reprint, New York: Seven Stories Press, 1996.)

Twain, Mark. *Extract from Captain Stormfield's Visit to Heaven.* Introduction by Frederik Pohl, afterword by James A. Miller. In *The Oxford Mark Twain.* Edited by Shelley Fisher Fishkin. New York: Oxford University Press, 1996.

Vonnegut, Kurt. *Breakfast of Champions.* New York: Delta, 1999.

Vonnegut, Kurt. *The Sirens of Titan.* New York: Delta, 1998.

(Any of the other nearly twenty book-length works of fiction by Kurt Vonnegut are also recommended reading.)